poetry in motion from coast to coast

Also published by W. W. Norton & Company

Poetry in Motion: 100 Poems from the Subways and Buses,
edited by Elise Paschen, Molly Peacock, and Neil Neches

poetry in motion from coast to coast

One Hundred and Twenty Poems from the Subways and Buses

Edited by Elise Paschen and Brett Fletcher Lauer

Published in cooperation with the Poetry Society of America

Introduction by Elise Paschen

Preface by William Louis-Dreyfus

W. W. Norton & Company

New York | London

The text of this book is composed in Helvetica with the display set in Bubbledot
Composition by Julia Druskin
Manufacturing by The Courier Companies, Inc.
Book design and photographs by Blue Shoe Studio / Leelo Märjamaa-Reintal
Production manager: Amanda Morrison

Library of Congress Cataloging-in-Publication Data
Poetry in motion from coast to coast : 120 poems from the subways and buses / edited by Elise Paschen
and Brett Fletcher Lauer ; introduction by Elise Paschen ; Preface by William Louis-Dreyfus.
p. cm.
"Published in Cooperation with the Poetry Society of America."
Includes index.
ISBN 0-393-32376-5 (pbk.)
1. Poetry—Collections. I. Paschen, Elise. II. Lauer, Brett Fletcher. III. Poetry Socirty of America.
PN6101 .P54218 2002
808.81—dc21   2002071841

W. W. Norton & Company, Inc., 500 Fifth Avenue, New York, N.Y. 10110
www.wwnorton.com

W. W. Norton & Company Ltd., Castle House, 75/76 Wells Street, London W1T 3QT

1 2 3 4 5 6 7 8 9 0

table of contents

VIII

x

XII

XVI

XVIII

Preface

Of what use is poetry? There are accounts of conversations with Einstein in which he confidently leaves to poetry the answers to questions his physics could not find. But poetry contains no revealing formulas, no concrete information that can be applied to achieve an end, build a house, run a machine, construct a system. It was W. H. Auden who said that poetry could not make anything happen. So how does one explain the overriding place that poetry has in our human existence?

In 1992 MTA New York City Transit sought the help of the Poetry Society of America to install the *Poetry in Motion* program in its subways and buses. It obtained the enthusiastic cooperation of Molly Peacock and Elise Paschen, then the PSA's President and Executive Director. The PSA has since taken that program to the subways and buses of 11 other cities, fixing poems in the lines of sight and in the minds of people coming from and going to make things happen.

The poem stays observed by and observer of the enlivened human life full of incident around it. It echoes the felt and unsaid. It marks without revealing the mysteries of living. If the soul is a garden, then poetry is the seasons that encase it.

The *Poetry in Motion* program can only include short poems or excerpts from longer ones.

But there is emphasis in brevity, and a terse character is what made some thinkers choose English for the language of poets. It was Ben Jonson who said 400 years ago

In small proportions we just beauties see,
And in short measures life may perfect be.

The *Poetry in Motion* poems are like resting places along the road, each with its own portion of intimacy, calm, wisdom, and nourishment. In their display and gathering, poetry has found an additional use.

—William Louis-Dreyfus

Introduction

Americans from coast to coast have been discovering poems in the most unlikely places—in subway cars, in buses, even on billboards. On Washington, D.C.'s Red Line, it may be Walt Whitman's "When I Heard the Learn'd Astronomer"; on Chicago's elevated train, Gwendolyn Brooks's "We Real Cool"; while on Sunset Boulevard in Los Angeles a billboard flashes an excerpt of a poem by Pablo Neruda. For ten years now, *Poetry in Motion* placards have appeared in the transit systems of a dozen cities across the country, reaching over thirteen million people a day.

Bringing poems back into everyday life is a goal of the Poetry Society of America (PSA). Founded in 1910, the Poetry Society is the country's oldest national poetry organization, but in its long history no other program has sparked the public's imagination the way *Poetry in Motion* has. It has touched many people who don't ordinarily read poetry, and hundreds have written letters explaining why. One New York City subway rider even commented: "I look forward to riding the subway because I know I'm going to discover a very special poem that will add meaning to my life."

Poetry in Motion was inspired by a similar program in London called *Poems on the Underground*. On a Poetry Society reading tour of England with Native American women poets,

I spotted a sonnet by Michael Drayton on the London Tube and fantasized about featuring poems on subways cars and buses in New York City. Around the same time, Alan Kiepper, then President of MTA New York City Transit, also visiting England, became inspired by the notion of poems on public transportation and decided a similar program should appear in New York's subways and buses. MTA New York City Transit contacted the Poetry Society and, since 1992, the PSA has collaborated with MTA NYC Transit on *Poetry in Motion* in New York City.

Because of the great success of the New York City program, the Poetry Society decided to extend *Poetry in Motion* nationally. Since 1996, thanks to partnerships with local transit authorities and other institutions, the PSA has launched *Poetry in Motion* in numerous cities across the country. Chicagoans first celebrated *Poetry in Motion* in 1996 with "Chicago Loves Poetry," a Valentine's Day extravaganza at the Harold Washington Library, broadcast on Chicago Cable TV. In 1997, we cohosted a poetry festival in Portland's Pioneer Courthouse Square with a bus filled with *Poetry in Motion* posters. Before long *Poetry in Motion* began appearing in subway cars and buses in Atlanta, Austin, Baltimore, Boston, Dallas, Fort Collins, Houston, Iowa City, Los Angeles, Philadelphia, Pioneer Valley, Mass., and Washington, D.C.

Poetry in Motion from Coast to Coast is a sequel to *Poetry in Motion: 100 Poems from the Subways and Buses.* In the earlier book we published the first 100 poems that appeared on New York's subways and buses, while this new anthology features a selection of poems from the PSA's national program. In choosing poems for each city, we attempt to represent poets from that particular region as well as include acclaimed national and international poets from different eras. Because the poem has to fit on a subway or bus placard, we select short poems though, in some instances, we do excerpt from longer ones (indicated in the table of contents by the word *from*). We aspire to reach people from all backgrounds and of all ages—so we present poems in a variety of styles and genres and from many cultures, including bilingual car cards featuring foreign poems in their original language and in English.

In selecting these poems over the past decade, we have collaborated with many regional partners. (We have attempted to thank them all in the acknowledgments. We also owe special gratitude to Molly Peacock, a cofounder of *Poetry in Motion*; to Alice Quinn, Executive Director of the PSA; and to our former *Poetry in Motion* coordinators.) But in every case it always seemed clear what represented a striking *Poetry in Motion* poem: a poem that stops the heart and arrests the attention, yet also a poem that may be rediscovered over repeated readings in the crowded world of a commuter's day.

Instead of arranging the anthology geographically, or city by city, we decided to assemble the poems thematically—opening the book with beginnings (whether of the day or of time itself) and concluding when night descends and stars emerge. In the table of contents we have indicated beneath each poet's name the city or cities in which the poem originally appeared on a bus or subway poster. Those cities that sponsored *Poetry in Motion* for many years are, naturally, represented by the most poems.

None of the poems from our first *Poetry in Motion* anthology are reprinted in this book. We also could not publish every poem that appeared in all the subway cars and buses across the country, so we narrowed down our selection to a sampling of 120 poems from twelve cities. This anthology offers a feast of poems from across America. We hope you will savor each one!

—Elise Paschen

poetry in motion from coast to coast

from Emergence

A human mind is small when thinking
of small things.
It is large when embracing the maker
of walking, thinking and flying.
If I can locate the sense beyond desire,
I will not eat or drink
until I stagger into the earth
with grief.
I will locate the point of dawning
and awaken
with the longest day in the world.

JOY HARJO (b. 1951)

Naming the Animals

Having commanded Adam to bestow
Names upon all creatures, God withdrew
To empyrean palaces of blue
That warm and windless morning long ago,
And seemed to take no notice of the vexed
Look on the young man's face as he took thought
Of all the miracles the Lord had wrought,
Now to be labelled, dubbed, yclept, indexed.

Before an addled mind and puddled brow,
The feathered nation and the finny prey
Passed by; there went biped and quadruped.
Adam looked forth with bottomless dismay

Into the tragic eyes of his first cow,
And shyly ventured, "Thou shalt be called 'Fred.'"

ANTHONY HECHT (b. 1923)

Ceres Looks at the Morning

I wake slowly. Already
my body is a twilight: Solid. Cold.
At the edge of a larger darkness. But outside
my window
a summer day is beginning. Apple trees
appear, one by one. Light is pouring
into the promise of fruit.

                           Beautiful morning
look at me as a daughter would
look: with that love and that curiosity:
as to what she came from.
And what she will become.

EAVAN BOLAND (b. 1944)

The Sonogram

Only a few weeks ago, the sonogram of Jean's womb
resembled nothing so much
as a satellite-map of Ireland:

now the image
is so well-defined we can make out not only a hand
but a thumb;

on the road to Spiddal, a woman hitching a ride;
a gladiator in his net, passing judgment on the crowd.

PAUL MULDOON (b. 1951)

Blackberries

The birthing scream uncoiled
across the grass, catching in our throats,
in our blackberry purple fingertips.

We came from the fields scratched and brown
buckets of berries under our arms.
My baby sister was born covered

in clotted milk, and we stood wide eyed
at the edge of the room, clenching our buckets in our fists.
Through the window, the August sun turned dust motes

to flecks of gold, and flung light through the cream walled room.
Father tied the eerie blue cord with a string,
and we buried the placenta beneath the cherry tree.

GABRIELE HAYDEN (b. 1979)

First Early Mornings Together

Waking up over the candy store together
We hear birds waking up below the sill
And slowly recognize ourselves, the weather,
The time, and the birds that rustle there until

Down to the street as fog and quiet lift
The pigeons from the wrinkled awning flutter
To reconnoiter, mutter, stare and shift
Pecking by ones or twos the rainbowed gutter.

ROBERT PINSKY (b. 1940)

from Art: African-American Woman Guild, or
The Spider Explains Her Art to the Blind

I am the singer with no name
fine-tuning screams to grace that keens
crisscrossing in the sky.

10

I am the cradling star stripping devils before morning.

I am an angel on the head of a pin.
No one can count these steps.

I am spinning earth's axis.

I am lotus sitting in the lion's mouth.

I am breathing in a silver bell.

I am beaming in the doorway.
Either come inside or
Get out of my light.

ANGELA JACKSON (b. 1951)

Sonnet XXIX

When, in disgrace with fortune and men's eyes,
I all alone beweep my outcast state,
And trouble deaf heaven with my bootless cries,
And look upon myself and curse my fate,
Wishing me like to one more rich in hope,
Featured like him, like him with friends possessed,
Desiring this man's art, and that man's scope,
With what I most enjoy contented least;
Yet in these thoughts myself almost despising,
Haply I think on thee—and then my state,
Like to the lark at break of day arising
From sullen earth, sings hymns at heaven's gate,
For thy sweet love remembered such wealth brings
That then I scorn to change my state with kings.

WILLIAM SHAKESPEARE (1564–1616)

12

Red Rooster, Yellow Sky

The grandmother who never spoke
brought me this card from Japan
drawn in a child's hand:
just rooster, sun, and sky.
Under a red sun
the rooster's red body
splits in two uneven parts,
each sturdy black foot
holding its own weight.
It was the year of the rooster
when I was still ten,
learning to stand myself upright—
my own sky rising yellow
like new, uncut lemons.

AMY UYEMATSU

Beautiful Days

Blossoms lift the branches
So the birds move.

The first leaves shine.

These are nice days, shipshape and fair.
Birds over all
Are moving.

But then I think, they
Are happy and gay,

They do not know
What life does.

MARY KINZIE (b. 1944)

14

from **Sympathy**

I know why the caged bird sings, ah me,
   When his wing is bruised and his bosom sore, —
When he beats his bars and he would be free;
It is not a carol of joy or glee,
   But a prayer that he sends from his heart's deep core,
But a plea, that upward to Heaven he flings —
I know why the caged bird sings!

PAUL LAURENCE DUNBAR (1872–1906)

False Spring

an uncanny raucous chirp chirp is heard
as mockful birds suddenly appear making nests
quarrelsome with unexpected matings
and the heady blush of bugs 'n such stir 'n sting anew
enthralled lovers stroll neath a startled blue sky
hayfever aroused prematurely by the lusty santanas
blinds me with sneeze
and my restless lay moves on to moister ground
(and they say i've never known snow)
it is the middle of winter California-style
tell that to the magenta butterflies
blossoms pink and yellow limbs bared scanty weeks ago
even the trees are deceived

WANDA COLEMAN (b. 1946)

from Eruption: Pu'u O'o

Novices, we dressed and drove out,
first to the crater rim, Uwekahuna
a canyon and sea of ash and moonstone,
the hardened, grey back of Leviathan
steaming and venting, dormant under cloud-cover.
And then next down Volcano Road past the villages
to Hirano Store on Kilauea's long plateau.
There, over canefield and the hardened lava land,
all we saw was in each other's eyes—
the mind's fear and the heart's delight,
running us this way and that.

GARRETT HONGO (b. 1951)

from **Foreign Exchange**

How can a person make herself go to work,
drive the car, wash her hair, change her
clothes, get up, sit down, get up again,
and so on, without a kiss to break up
the monotony? Sometimes it's impossible to go on
without a kiss, as if your life were a run-on
sentence, as if your life were the Berlin Wall
with soldiers guarding your openings,
as if there were not enough mouths
to go around in the village, and your lips
were swollen with hunger
scrabbling with your sister for one dried-up
kiss the size of a silver dollar.

MARION WINIK (b. 1958)

Espresso

Black coffee at sidewalk cafés
with chairs and tables like gaudy insects.

It is a precious sip we intercept
filled with the same strength as Yes and No.

It is fetched out of gloomy kitchens
and looks into the sun without blinking.

In daylight a dot of wholesome black
quickly drained by the wan patron . . .

Like those black drops of profundity
sometimes absorbed by the soul

that give us a healthy push: Go!
The courage to open our eyes.

TOMAS TRANSTRÖMER (b. 1931)
Translated from the Swedish by May Swenson and Leif Sjöberg

Peaches

A mouthful of language to swallow:
stretches of beach, sweet clinches,
breaches in walls, pleached branches;
britches hauled over haunches;
hunched leeches, wrenched teachers.
What English can do: ransack
the warmth that chuckles beneath
fuzzed surfaces, smooth velvet
richness, plashy juices.
I beseech you, peach,
clench me into the sweetness
of your reaches.

PETER DAVISON (b. 1928)

Walking to School, 1964

Blurring the window, the snowflakes' numb white lanterns.
She's brewed her coffee, in the bathroom sprays cologne
And sets her lipstick upright on the sink.
The door ajar, I glimpse the yellow slip,

The rose-colored birthmark on her shoulder.
Then she's dressed—the pillbox hat and ersatz fur,
And I'm dressed too, mummified in stocking cap
And scarves, and I walk her to the bus stop

Where she'll leave me for my own walk to school,
Where she'll board the bus that zigzags to St. Paul
As I watch her at the window, the paperback

Romance already open on her lap,

The bus laboring off into snow, her good-bye kiss
Still startling my cheek with lipstick trace.

DAVID WOJAHN (b. 1953)

Lilac Time

The winter was fierce, my dear,
      Snowy and blowy and cold,
A heart-breaker and record-breaker,
      And I am feeble and old.

But now it is lilac time.
      Come out in the sweet warm air,
Come and I'll gather flowers
      To put in your beautiful hair.

Let's make a bouquet of lilac
      For our old bedside table.
Then the fragrance in the night
      Will make me form-i-dable.

HAYDEN CARRUTH (b. 1921)

24

from **The World Is Round**

I am Rose my eyes are blue
I am Rose and who are you
I am Rose and when I sing
I am Rose like anything

GERTRUDE STEIN (1874–1946)

Riddle

We are animal cries,
groans the body makes,
the shrill keening of grief,
pain and rage howled out,
grunts of satisfaction,
someone crooning to her young.
We're animal cries becoming
human, five daughters
of your mother tongue.

[Answer: Vowels]

NAN FRY (b. 1945)

26

A Tin Roof Song

The music is a tap dancer's sliding soft shoe,
a regimen of holy roller churches where pastors hold
the pulpit swinging the other hand freely, receiving
the Holy Ghost descending. In the house the music
settles frazzled, black farmers—in Africa under
the stupor, the glaze of hunger, in America under
a driving will to be. Harder the rain falls,
darker the night rolls beneath a moon
full of memories, ancestral. Music from rain incites us
to dance, clay-stained, black toes wiggle in sleep to thunder,
a steady slurping of rain falling in sand,
a slow clap of wooden screen doors as dogs retreat.
Lightning cracks on far sides of fields,
splitting edges of forests, lighting tree tops.
An unfamiliar ritual has begun, a past is incarnate,

a West African mask with eyes like black lips
mounted on a sleek, doll body for its divination—
it is the soul of our fathers and mothers.

AFAA MICHAEL WEAVER (b. 1951)

from **The Choice**

Sundays,

she listened to the church choir
hold their long whole notes. Everything
had a knack for hanging on.
Even the old refrigerator
by the kitchen table, though it
shook with noise like a train,
wasn't going anywhere.

But in the tailor shop downstairs
where things are made right,
garments were left hanging,
what is human set free again
from the arms of cloth.

ELAINE TERRANOVA (b. 1939)

from **Avalanche**

this poem waits for you to cross over
to cross over the heartbeat touch of your healing
hands, touching hands, touching hearts
this poem waits for you to cross over
to cross over love, this poem waits for you
to cross over, to cross over love
this poem waits for you to crossover
too crossover, too, love

QUINCY TROUPE (b. 1943)

Days of Our Years

It's brief and bright, dear children; bright and brief.
Delight's the lightning; the long thunder's grief.

JOHN FREDERICK NIMS (1913–1999)

At Noon

The thick-walled room's cave-darkness,
cool in summer, soothes
by saying, This is the Truth, not the taut
cicada-strummed daylight.
Rest here, out of the flame—the thick air's
stirred by the fan's four
slow-moving spoons; under the house the stone
has its feet in deep water.
Outside, even the sun god, dressed in this life
as a lizard, abruptly rises
on stiff legs and descends blasé toward the shadows.

REGINALD GIBBONS (b. 1947)

El Chicle
(for Marcel)

Mi'jo and I were laughing—*ha, ha, ha*—
when the gum he chewed fell out of his mouth
and into my hair which, after I clipped it,
flew in the air, on the back of a dragonfly
that dipped in the creek and was snapped fast
by a turtle that reached high and swam deep.
Mi'jo wondered what happened to that gum,
worried that it stuck to the back
of my seat and Mami will be mad when
she can't get it out. Meanwhile,
the turtle in the pond that ate the dragonfly
that carried the hair
with the gum on its back

swam South and hasn't been seen once
since.

ANA CASTILLO (b. 1953)

34

I Ask My Mother to Sing

She begins, and my grandmother joins her.
Mother and daughter sing like young girls.
If my father were alive, he would play
his accordion and sway like a boat.

I've never been in Peking, or the Summer Palace,
nor stood on the great Stone Boat to watch
the rain begin on Kuen Ming Lake, the picnickers
running away in the grass.

But I love to hear it sung;
how the waterlilies fill with rain until
they overturn, spilling water into water,
then rock back, and fill with more.

Both women have begun to cry,
But neither stops her song.

LI-YOUNG LEE (b. 1957)

The Cure

Here she is

with me again, too deep in bottle-green seawater,
featureless and elongated, spread out

symmetrically, a blue and sand starfish, my laughing
and angry and smoking and way lovely daughter.

Wrist by wrist and half blind we hold on so hard
to each other that every last islet of Langerhans

fuses, zapped somehow functional
and rejection proof *yes* as we plunge

out of air toward the surface *won't make it* footlessly
kicking and already missing each other and desperate,

and breathe.

JAMES McMANUS (b. 1951)

38

A Poem for Jesse

your face like
summer lightning
gets caught in my voice
and i draw you up from
deep rivers
taste your face of a
thousand names
see you smile
a new season
hear your voice
a wild sea pausing in the wind.

SONIA SANCHEZ (b. 1934)

39

from **Praise the Tortilla, Praise Menudo, Praise Chorizo**

I praise the chorizo and smear it across
my face and hands, the dayglow brown of it
painting me with desire to find out why
the chorizo sizzled in the pan and covered the house
with a smell of growing up I will never have again,
the chorizo burrito hot in my hands
when I ran out to play and show the vatos
it was time to cut the chorizo,
tell it like it is before *la manteca* runs
down our chins and drips away.

RAY GONZALEZ (b. 1952)

40

Wrong Side of the River

I watched you on the wrong side
of the river, waving. You were trying
to tell me something. You used both hands
and sort of ran back and forth,
as if to say *look behind you, look out
behind you.* I wanted to wave back.
But you began shouting and I didn't
want you to think I understood.
So I did nothing but stand still,
thinking that's what to do on the wrong side
of the river. After a while you did too.
We stood like that for a long time. Then
I raised a hand, as if to be called on,
and you raised a hand, as if to the same question.

STANLEY PLUMLY (b. 1939)

Ventanas Pintadas

Vivía en una casa
con dos ventanas de verdad y las otras dos pintadas en la fachada.
Aquellas ventanas pintadas fueron mi primer dolor.
Palpaba las paredes del pasillo,
intentando encontrar las ventanas por dentro.
Toda mi infancia la pasé con el deseo
de asomarme para ver lo que se veía
desde aquellas ventanas que no existieron.

Painted Windows

I lived in a house
with two real windows and the other two painted on.
Those painted windows caused my first sorrow.
I'd touch the sides of the hall
trying to reach the windows from inside.
I spent my whole childhood wanting
to lean out and see what could be seen
from the windows that weren't there.

GLORIA FUERTES (1918–1998)
Translated from the Spanish by Philip Levine

Cow Worship

I love the cows best when they are a few feet away
from my dining-room window and my pine floor,
when they reach in to kiss me with their wet
mouths and their white noses.
I love them when they walk over the garbage cans
and across the cellar doors,
over the sidewalk and through the metal chairs
and the birdseed.
—Let me reach out through the thin curtains
and feel the warm air of May.
It is the temperature of the whole galaxy,
all the bright clouds and clusters,
beasts and heroes,
glittering singers and isolated thinkers
at pasture.

GERALD STERN (b. 1925)

The Loon on Oak-Head Pond

cries for three days, in the gray mist.
cries for the north it hopes it can find.

plunges, and comes up with a slapping pickerel.
blinks its red eye.

cries again.

you come every afternoon, and wait to hear it.
you sit a long time, quiet, under the thick pines,
in the silence that follows.

as though it were your own twilight.
as though it were your own vanishing song.

MARY OLIVER (b. 1935)

The Eagle

He clasps the crag with crooked hands;
Close to the sun in lonely lands,
Ringed with the azure world, he stands.

The wrinkled sea beneath him crawls;
He watches from his mountain walls,
And like a thunderbolt he falls.

ALFRED, LORD TENNYSON (1809–1892)

from A Chorus of Horizontals

Wherever you go those geese follow, slick Harpies, as if you're
their star, their hunger. They all point to you. You believe this

and it keeps you alive through winter after winter when, missing them,
you go down to the steely Chicago at the end of your ice-encrusted

impossible street and throw bread upon the water.

MAUREEN SEATON (b. 1947)

from **Of Pairs**

The mockingbirds, that pair, arrive,
one, and the other; glossily perch,
respond, respond, branch to branch.
One stops, and flies. The other flies.
Arrives, dips, in a blur of wings,
lights, is joined. Sings. Sings.

Actually, there are birds galore:
bowlegged blackbirds brassy as crows;
elegant ibises with inelegant cows;
hummingbirds' stutter on air;
tilted over the sea, a man-of-war
in a long arc without a feather's stir.

JOSEPHINE JACOBSEN (b. 1908)

Keeping Things Whole

In a field
I am the absence
of field.
This is
always the case.
Wherever I am
I am what is missing.

When I walk
I part the air
and always
the air moves in
to fill the spaces
where my body's been.

We all have reasons
for moving.
I move
to keep things whole.

MARK STRAND (b. 1934)

50

Milkweed

While I stood here, in the open, lost in myself,
I must have looked a long time
Down the corn rows, beyond grass,
The small house,
White walls, animals lumbering toward the barn.
I look down now. It is all changed.
Whatever it was I lost, whatever I wept for
Was a wild, gentle thing, the small dark eyes
Loving me in secret.
It is here. At a touch of my hand,
The air fills with delicate creatures
From the other world.

JAMES WRIGHT (1927–1980)

The Bears

My brother saw the amorous bears
rolling about in the meadow up by
Lowder Mountain—the lupine crushed,
paintbrush flattened in their
loving swathe—how he nibbled
her ear and she smacked him
with her paw, there in the fall
of fat September. And my brother
crept away on hands and knees
into the hemlock thicket.
Then the rain, the snow, and we
in our separate lives content
because sunlight struck a pair
of bears apart from our human way—

this wearing of shoes, and words,
and nations.

KIM STAFFORD (b. 1949)

from Poppies

I was Alice pursuing the white rabbit.
When I put my foot in a hole and tumbled down
I was Jack with an empty pail of water.
Waiting for the pain to let up I imagined
Around the World in 80 Days,
My ankle soaring as crowds cheered.
Oh yes there were moments of delight,
Stories I felt a sure part of,
Days in which you and I were perfect.

ROBERT McDOWELL (b. 1953)

In Between

Once, our bodies were bells:
Simply moving in the wind
We tolled our names.

PHILLIS LEVIN (b. 1954)

The Tree House

Have you seen our mulberry tree
And the neighborhood children
With purple lips and blue fingers
Climbing to the house
In its branches?

MAY MILLER (1899–1995)

On the Patio, Dallas

The prickly pear and yucca
dug from a roadside
do fine in pots. Sun,
sunflowers. The August heat.
Petunias, pinks, and even the geranium
probably don't belong. With watering
they hold on. One morning
I fed them Ortho Fertilizer
made entirely of sea-going fish.
I hosed the place till the hanging baskets
dripped and the fence soaked dark.
There rose the brackish smell of bays
and wharves and I turned my head

to the distance as if to hear
the regular slapping of the sea.

ISABEL NATHANIEL (b. 1940)

from **Untitled**

There is no First or Last
Only equality
And who would rule
Joins the majority.
There is no Space or Time
Only intensity,
And tame things
Have no immensity.

MINA LOY (1882–1966)

from **Brotherly Love**

And they shall come together in a city,

> City of lovely purposes
> upholding balconies
> espaliered on walls
> and windows
> reeling with cerulean light—

> where each breath's an anthem and each glance a hymn,
> here is the spirit's home.

DANIEL HOFFMAN (b. 1923)

60

We Real Cool

**The Pool Players.
Seven at the Golden Shovel.**

We real cool. We
Left school. We

Lurk late. We
Strike straight. We

Sing sin. We
Thin gin. We

Jazz June. We
Die soon.

GWENDOLYN BROOKS (1917–2000)

I Finally Managed to Speak to Her

She was sitting across from me
on the bus. I said, "The trees
look so much greener in this part
of the country. In New York City
everything looks so drab." She said,
"It looks the same to me. Show me
a tree that's different." "That one,"
I said. "Which one?" she said.
"It's too late," I said; "we already
passed it." "When you find another one,"
she said, "let me know." And then
she went back to reading her book.

HAL SIROWITZ (b. 1949)

from My Grandmother's New York Apartment

Everything pulled out or folded away:
sofa into a bed, tray tables that dis-
appear behind a door, everything
transmutable, alchemy in small
spaces, even my grandmother tiny
and changeable: a housecoat and rollers
which vanish and become an Irish
tweed suit, a tilted chapeau, a Hello
in the elevator just like, as she
would say, the Queen of Denmark.

ELIZABETH ALEXANDER (b. 1962)

Hanging the Wash

Mama said you could always tell
the state of a woman's love life
by the condition of her underwear.
Twenty ivory briefs
flapping in the wind,
not a lavender, pink,
or naughty black
in the whole sensible lot.
Four beige half slips like
neutral guards in a row.
No touch of scarlet or
little pink rosettes,

just clean drawers hanging
on a gray metal clothes line.

Oh, Mama, how did you ever learn so much?

CYNTHIA HARPER (b. 1948)

Instruction

My hands that guide a needle
In their turn are led
Relentlessly and deftly
As a needle leads a thread.

Other hands are teaching
My needle: when I sew
I feel the cool, thin fingers
Of hands I do not know.

They urge my needle onward.
They smooth my seams, until
The worry of my stitches
Smothers in their skill.

All the tired women,
Who sewed their lives away,
Speak in my deft fingers
As I sew to-day.

HAZEL HALL (1886–1924)

Lineage

My grandmothers were strong.
They followed plows and bent to toil.
They moved through fields sowing seed.
They touched earth and grain grew.
They were full of sturdiness and singing.
My grandmothers were strong.

My grandmothers are full of memories
Smelling of soap and onions and wet clay
With veins rolling roughly over quick hands
They have many clean words to say.
My grandmothers were strong.
Why am I not as they?

MARGARET WALKER (1915–1998)

The Courage of Women

I think of the courage of women,
      how they endure,
how they walk miles to carry back water,
silence their pain, apportion
what's left of the rice.
      Keepers of eggs without shells,
they know how fragile the days are,
        how hope can spill into the ground.

JANE GLAZER (b. 1925)

The Hands

The poor hands, overworked and dry,
dressing the body like maids
who button the lady's silk shirt
and fan her with their palms.

70

The poor palms
with their geography of lines.
One is broken,
another tells us, short life.

It is just like the hands
to tell their stories without shame.
Even held down, the white knucklebones
assert themselves through the skin.

LINDA HOGAN (b. 1947)

Open House

I work as hard as I can
to have nothing to do.

Birds climb their rich ladder
of choruses.

They have tasted the top of the tree,
but they are not staying.

The whole sky says,
Your move.

NAOMI SHIHAB NYE (b. 1952)

Too Much Heat, Too Much Work

It's the fourteenth of August, and I'm too hot
To endure food, or bed. Steam and the fear of scorpions
Keep me awake. I'm told the heat won't fade with Autumn.

Swarms of flies arrive. I'm roped into my clothes.
In another moment I'll scream down the office
As the paper mountains rise higher on my desk.

Oh those real mountains to the south of here!
I gaze at the ravines kept cool by pines.
If I could walk on ice, with my feet bare!

TU FU (712–770)
Translated from the Chinese by Carolyn Kizer

The Potter's Wheel

for Jane

I was mindless
As a lump of clay, drunk on gin
Until my kidneys ached,

The summer I met you.
I was the child, also master
With as many heads as a totem-pole;
But I denied you maternal

Pleasures by alternating my roles
Like a double agent.
Each time I'm almost forgotten I rise
Unexpectedly like a monadnock.

Soft in the center,
A blunt man whose life flattens
Near the edges,

I grow in your hands.
Everything changes except the shape
You give me.

74

CALVIN FORBES (b. 1945)

from Mending Wall

Before I built a wall I'd ask to know
What I was walling in or walling out,
And to whom I was like to give offense.
Something there is that doesn't love a wall,
That wants it down.

ROBERT FROST (1874–1963)

from **Heavy Tells a Story**

When Heavy tells a story
the millwright shanty under the electric furnaces
chokes with quiet, amid the roar,
as Heavy pauses, adjusts his mountainous weight
over a creaky grease-stained metal chair
and looks up at the whirling ceiling fan
next to fluorescent lights hanging by wires.
His fingers lace like so many sausages
across the canvas of blue workshirt
on his chest.

LUIS J. RODRIGUEZ (b. 1954)

The Mill Back Home

Logs drowse in the pond
Dreaming of their heroes
Alligator and crocodile

VERN RUTSALA (b. 1934)

Confusion

When confusion reigns
and the waitress begins to think
that the hungry exist for her,
and the air hostess begins to think
that the passengers exist for her,
and the pharmacist begins to think
that the patient exists for her,
and the reviewer begins to think
that the author exists for her—
and not the other way about:

When confusion reigns
I too, my love, begin to think
that you were made for me.

NINO NIKOLOV (b. 1933)
Translated from the Bulgarian by Ewald Osers

from **Auburn**

Your auburn hair
over my fingers—runs away.

A ribboned shore, designs awake
by strange mountains . . .

I know of a stream.
Sway me in its olive smoke.

Lift the curled leaves—
a pebbled shawl for its tiny trees.

Bring me your careful notebooks.
Boyhood calligrams. Remember

when we found a yellow-green
pinecone and you said it was the earth
with a spike shoe, a spike dress?
Slip away from the marbled cliff.

You
with a raging spiral heart.

80

JUAN FELIPE HERRERA (b. 1948)

Epigram V, xxxvi

Someone I flattered in a book pretends
he owes me nothing. Oh the trash I have for friends!

Laudatus nostro quidam, Faustine, libello
dissimulat, quasi nil debeat: inposuit.

MARTIAL (40–104)
Translated from the Latin by William Matthews

The Door

the day after the national election
the sky cleared and the sun found its guitar.
i ran to the plaza and soon discovered myself
dancing in the middle of a jubilant crowd.
a nation of song, a nation of thousands pushing
like the sea to the cathedral. i felt the sweet
sweat of arms, legs and chests. i found my place
among the living, the dead, the ghosts, the children
waiting to be born. something more powerful than
victory was in the air. i could breathe again.
my prison door was open. my country was outside.
she had been waiting for me.

E. ETHELBERT MILLER (b. 1950)

The Grade-School Angels

None of us understood the dark secret of the blackboards
nor why the armillary sphere seemed so remote when we looked at it.
We knew only that a circumference does not have to be round
and that an eclipse of the moon confuses the flowers
and speeds up the timing of birds.

None of us understood anything:
not even why our fingers were made of India ink
and the afternoon closed compasses only to have the dawn open books.
We knew only that a straight line, if it likes, can be curved or broken
and that the wandering stars are children who don't know arithmetic.

RAFAEL ALBERTI (1902–1999)
Translated from the Spanish by Mark Strand

from **Daily Horoscope**

4. Beware of things in duplicate . . .

Beware of things in duplicate:
a set of knives, the cufflinks in a drawer,
the dice, the pair of Queens, the eyes
of someone sitting next to you.
Attend that empty minute in the evening
when looking at the clock, you see
its hands are fixed on the same hour
you noticed at your morning coffee.
These are the moments to beware
when there is nothing so familiar
or so close that it cannot betray you:
a twin, an extra key, an echo,
your own reflection in the glass.

DANA GIOIA (b. 1950)

84

The Whistle

You could whistle me home from anywhere
in the neighborhood; avenues away,
I'd pick out your clear, alternating pair
of notes, the signal to quit my child's play
and run back to our house for supper,
or a Saturday trip to the hardware store.
Unthrottled, wavering in the upper
reaches, your trilled summons traveled farther
than our few blocks. I've learned too, how your heart's
radius extends, though its beat
has stopped. Still, some days a sudden fear darts
through me, whether it's my own city street
I hurry across, or at a corner in an unknown
town: the high, vacant air arrests me—*where's home?*

KATHY MANGAN (b. 1950)

whose side are you on?

the side of the busstop woman
trying to drag her bag
up the front steps before the doors
clang shut   i am on her side
i give her exact change
and him the old man hanging by
one strap his work hand folded shut
as the bus doors i am on his side
when he needs to leave
i ring the bell   i am on their side
riding the late bus into the same
someplace   i am on the dark side always
the side of my daughters
the side of my tired sons

LUCILLE CLIFTON (b. 1936)

Hunger

The fox you lug over your shoulder
in a dark sack
has cut a hole with a knife
and escaped.

The sudden lightness makes you think
you are stronger
as you walk back to your small cottage
through a forest that covers the world.

BILLY COLLINS (b. 1941)

from **Men at Forty**

At rest on a stair landing,
They feel it moving
Beneath them now like the deck of a ship,
Though the swell is gentle.

And deep in mirrors
They rediscover
The face of the boy as he practices tying
His father's tie there in secret,

And the face of that father,
Still warm with the mystery of lather.
They are more fathers than sons themselves now.

DONALD JUSTICE (b. 1925)

from Commuter Marriage

Home. My eyes were full of tears
as I handed my obol to the ferryman,
my quarter to the woman at the tolls,
and took the last, familiar stretch of road.
There's the all-night donut stand, the endless
chainlink fence bounding the airport field,
there's my favorite beech tree. There at last
our small green townhouse propped between its neighbors.
Oh lighted windows, darkling silhouette
where someone stands against them, waiting to hear
the crunch of gravel and the motor's hush.
So long, so far. I missed you very much.

EMILY GROSHOLZ (b. 1950)

Sonnet

A man talking to his ex-wife on the phone.
He has loved her voice and listens with attention
to every modulation of its tone. Knowing
it intimately. Not knowing what he wants
from the sound of it, from the tendered civility.
He studies, out the window, the seed shapes
of the broken pods of ornamental trees.
The kind that grow in everyone's garden, that no one
but horticulturists can name. Four arched chambers
of pale green, tiny vegetal proscenium arches,
a pair of black tapering seeds bedded in each chamber.
A wish geometry, miniature, Indian or Persian,
lovers or gods in their apartments. Outside, white,
patient animals, and tangled vines, and rain.

ROBERT HASS (b. 1941)

Paper Matches

My aunts washed dishes while the uncles
squirted each other on the lawn with
   garden hoses. Why are we in here,
I said, and they are out there?
   That's the way it is,
   said Aunt Hetty, the shriveled-up one.

   I have the rages that small animals have,
being small, being animal.
   Written on me was a message,
"At Your Service,"
like a book of paper matches.
One by one we were taken out
and struck.
   We come bearing supper,
our heads on fire.

PAULETTE JILES (b. 1943)

from **Fences**

I write in English, dream
in Spanish, listen to Latin chants.
I like streets where
Chicanos make up words.
Sometimes, I shout
Italian words to wake
the morning light.
At dusk, I breathe out
fragments of Swahili.
I want to feel words
swimming in my throat
like fighting fish
that refuse to be hooked
on a line.

BENJAMIN ALIRE SÁENZ (b. 1954)

from **Crazy Horse Speaks**

I wear the color of my skin
like a brown paper bag
wrapped around a bottle.
Sleeping between
the pages of dictionaries
your language cuts
tears holes in my tongue
until I do not have strength
to use the word "love."
What could it mean
in this city where everyone is
Afraid-of-Horses?

SHERMAN ALEXIE (b. 1966)

Comunicación

Yo te hablo de poesía
y vos me preguntás
a qué hora comemos.
Lo peor es que
yo también tengo hambre.

94

Communication

I am talking to you about poetry
and you say
when do we eat.
The worst of it is
I'm hungry too.

ALICIA PARTNOY (b. 1955)
Translated from the Spanish by Richard Schaaf, Regina Kreger, and the author

Love Like Salt

It lies in our hands in crystals
too intricate to decipher

It goes into the skillet
without being given a thought

It spills on the floor, so fine
we step all over it

We carry a pinch behind each eyeball

It breaks out on our foreheads

We store it inside our bodies
in secret wineskins

At supper, we pass it around the table
talking of holidays by the sea

LISEL MUELLER (b. 1924)

from **Misgivings**

Listen,
my wary one, it's far too late
to unlove each other. Instead let's cook
something elaborate and not
invite anyone to share it but eat it
all up very very slowly.

WILLIAM MATTHEWS (1942–1997)

from **Happy Family**

Tonight, the waiter brings Happy Family
steaming under a metal dome
and three small igloos of rice.
Mounded on the white oval plate, the unlikely
marriage of meat and fish, crab and chicken.
Not all Happy Families are alike.
The chef's tossed in wilted greens
and water chestnuts, silk against crunch;
he's added fresh ginger to baby corn,
carrots, bamboo shoots, scallions, celery,
broccoli, pea pods, bok choy.
My daughter impales a chunk of beef
on her chopstick and contentedly

sucks on it, like a popsicle.
Eating Happy Family, we all begin to smile.

JANE SHORE (b. 1947)

Primitive

I have heard about the civilized,
the marriages run on talk, elegant and
honest, rational. But you and I are
savages. You come in with a bag,
hold it out to me in silence.
I know Moo Shu Pork when I smell it
and understand the message: I have
pleased you greatly last night. We sit
quietly, side by side, to eat,
the long pancakes dangling and spilling,
fragrant sauce dripping out,
and glance at each other askance, wordless,
the corners of our eyes clear as spear points

laid along the sill to show
a friend sits with a friend here.

SHARON OLDS (b. 1942)

Harmonie du Soir

(Hampton's last concert in Santa Monica)

That ever younger evening sky's pastel accord's
A chord off Santa Monica
Even now, deepening shades of past
Shadings, jazzy, night jasmine's pungent fadings
In up from the Blue Virgin's blue
Through blues as interfused as tones in a harmonica
To cobalt blue, to coalfire blue, to Coltrane blue,
Smoky and chuffing, to blooming lavender of jacaranda
Flowers that fail, that fall across lanai, gazebo, and veranda,
Those years before your birth.

STEPHEN YENSER (b. 1941)

Sent on a Sheet of Paper with a Heart Shape Cut Out of the Middle of It

Empty, or open-hearted? Where
A full heart spoke once, now a strong
Outline is the most I dare:
A window opening onto fair
Shining meadows of hopefulness? Or long
Silence where there once was song,
Waves of remembrance in the darkening air.

JOHN HOLLANDER (b. 1929)

Scaffolding

Masons, when they start upon a building,
Are careful to test out the scaffolding;

Make sure that planks won't slip at busy points,
Secure all ladders, tighten bolted joints.

And yet all this comes down when the job's done
Showing off walls of sure and solid stone.

So if, my dear, there sometimes seem to be
Old bridges breaking between you and me

Never fear. We may let the scaffolds fall
Confident that we have built our wall.

SEAMUS HEANEY (b. 1939)

Delight in Disorder

A sweet disorder in the dress
Kindles in clothes a wantonness.
A lawn about the shoulders thrown
Into a fine distraction;
An erring lace, which here and there
Enthralls the crimson stomacher;
A cuff neglectful, and thereby
Ribbons to flow confusedly;
A winning wave, deserving note,
In the tempestuous petticoat;
A careless shoestring, in whose tie
I see a wild civility;
Do more bewitch me than when art
Is too precise in every part.

ROBERT HERRICK (1591–1674)

Separation

Your absence has gone through me
Like thread through a needle.
Everything I do is stitched with its color.

W. S. MERWIN (b. 1927)

from **Those Who Come After**

But when they say of us
what we have done, perhaps they will speak
kindly of those who, near the century's
end, pried open the hand;
of the way the wind lifted the lovely
gray spirals of ash, until our hands
were empty as a cloudless sky,
empty as altars whose offerings
had been acceptable; perhaps they will
say that there were those
who took down the harps
hung in the sorrowing trees, having lost
the taste for conquest or revenge,
and made a song

that rose in the air
as smoke rises—

ELEANOR WILNER (b. 1937)

Hysteria

I know I know
I took in too much
but the tree was there
with its enticing skins,
the garden intolerably quiet,
the snake so colorful, resolute,
I thought if I could just fondle
the fruit . . . but now, Please God,
I want to go back to the beginning
of the day so I can say no thank you:
it's all considerably more than I can handle.

SUSAN HAHN (b. 1941)

The Gift

For Bobby Jack Nelson

Older, more generous,
We give each other hope.
The gift is ominous:
Enough praise, enough rope.

N. SCOTT MOMADAY (b. 1934)

Tides

It's time to go, but still we sit
Lingering in our summer
Like idle fingers,
Like fingers in the sand.

Or like a tiny snail that moves
Beneath a gravelly pool,
Taking its life to travel,
Taking between the tides.

JOHN FULLER (b. 1937)

The Ideal

This is where I came from.
I passed this way.
This should not be shameful
Or hard to say.

A self is a self.
It is not a screen.
A person should respect
What he has been.

This is my past
Which I shall not discard.
This is the ideal.
This is hard.

JAMES FENTON (b. 1949)

This Is Just to Say

I have eaten
the plums
that were in
the icebox

and which
you were probably
saving
for breakfast

Forgive me
they were delicious
so sweet
and so cold

WILLIAM CARLOS WILLIAMS (1883–1963)

from **Little L.A. Villanelle**

I drove home that night in the rain.
The gutterless streets filled and overflowed.
After months of drought, the old refrain:

A cheap love song on the radio, off-key pain.
Through the maddening, humble gesture of the wipers,
I drove home that night in the rain.

I wanted another life, now it drives beside me
on the slick freeway, now it waves, faster, faster—
I drove home that night in the rain.
After months of drought, the old refrain.

CAROL MUSKE-DUKES (b. 1945)

Tower Suite

My father asked me, "Why do you write soft-sell?"
Cutting soft sole. "To sow hard seeds," I said,
"And sell hard souls." Through *The Tower* window,
The Time-Life sign blinked Time-Life, Time-Life
Flashing
Its occulting lights
Above the city.

GRACE SCHULMAN (b. 1935)

The Taxi

When I go away from you
The world beats dead
Like a slackened drum.
I call out for you against the jutted stars
And shout into the ridges of the wind.
Streets coming fast,
One after the other,
Wedge you away from me,
And the lamps of the city prick my eyes
So that I can no longer see your face.
Why should I leave you,
To wound myself upon the sharp edges of the night?

AMY LOWELL (1874–1925)

from **The Starlight Night**

Look at the stars! look, look up at the skies!
O look at all the fire-folk sitting in the air!

GERARD MANLEY HOPKINS (1844–1889)

118

from **Fireflies**

Too slow means a fast end,
a heavy hand, a jar
with holes punched in the lid,
a gathering of children
around the lights,
a milling of Chinese lanterns.
Cupped in my hand
one light fills my eye perfectly.
All evening I sit
on the porch swing and watch
not knowing where
the next will turn up—heat
lightning too far away
to hear.

JAMES McKEAN (b. 1946)

from In Spite of Everything, the Stars

Like a stunned piano, like a bucket
of fresh milk flung into the air
or a dozen fists of confetti
thrown hard at a bride
stepping down from the altar,
the stars surprise the sky.
Think of dazed stones
floating overhead, or an ocean
of starfish hung up to dry. Yes,
like a conductor's expectant arm
about to lift toward the chorus,
or a juggler's plates defying gravity,
or a hundred fastballs fired at once
and freezing in midair, the stars
startle the sky over the city.

EDWARD HIRSCH (b. 1950)

120

from The Heavy Light of Shifting Stars

The huge magnanimous stars are many things.
At night we lower the window shades
to mute the sparkling circuitry of the universe;
at day the sun's clear mist, like beautiful
cabinetry, shrouds the workings of the sky.

The huge magnanimous stars are many things.
We look to the sky and ask, What has changed?
Everything. But nothing we can see, and our seeing
changes nothing, until we move, and moving
we become the light of our atoms moving.

MICHAEL COLLIER (b. 1953)

The moonless night

The moonless night
the ice hill
the snow without shadows

are mine because
I need them.
I drive down the long slope

in first, waiting
to lose hold
and slip to the bottom.

They'll find the car
pulverized
and my shadow for shame.

But it all holds:
luck, gears—sand
to the stop sign.
Bless the sweet town grit!

ROSELLEN BROWN (b. 1939)

from **In February**

Sudden icy wind slaps at the ash
tree's thin frame; a shred of moon
hangs above clouds rushing east
over the lake.

Inside, I spread a hand
on the table, my palm
opening into slopes and ravines
of a weathered topography.

Going nowhere, I turn
in the night to reach among memories
that come apart, fade,
not caring

if they're no more than clouds
and belong to someone else's life.

RALPH J. MILLS, JR. (b. 1931)

White Towels

I have been studying the difference
between solitude and loneliness,
telling the story of my life
to the clean white towels taken warm from the dryer.
I carry them through the house
as though they were my children
asleep in my arms.

RICHARD JONES (b. 1953)

The Good Old Dog

I will lay down my silk robe
beside me near the old bed,
for the good old dog;
                  she loves the feel
of it under her, and she will
push it and pull it, knead
and scrape until she has it right;
                  then she'll drop down,
heavy, silver and black in the moonlight,
on it and a couple of pillows (not
bothering the cat who has taken over
                  her real bed)

                            and breathe out deeply.

Gorgeously fat,
her face
like the face of a seal.

TOI DERRICOTTE (b. 1941)

from **Rumors**

Some rivers remain questions, shifting
from side to side. Other questions
remain rivers, thick and muddy.
One bridge is a moth-eaten highway.
Another is a rhinestone bridge.

An architect wants to build a house
rivaling the mountains surrounding
his sleep, each turret mute as a hat.
He crosses a river to reach ground
hard enough to begin his plan. He crosses
a river the way a river crosses his sleep,
swirling with questions.

JOHN YAU (b. 1950)

Quies, or Rest

A woman goes from room to room. She extinguishes
One light in each room. Darkness follows her
And in the last room she is overtaken.
Then, she mounts the dark stair confidently
And enters the room she sleeps in, and lies
Down in the dark, where a man in the dark wakes
A little and covers her with his arm.

ALLEN GROSSMAN (b. 1932)

Lullaby for a Daughter

Someday, when the sands of time
invert, may you find perfect rest
as a newborn nurses from
the hourglass of your breast.

MARY JO SALTER (b. 1954)

0°

These nights when the wind blows,
I lay my head on the pillow,
I lay my head on white feathers,
white down, tag ends of Memory.
White feathers, white down,
I'm wrapped in a nightgown stiffening,
year by year, against the cold.
My arms hug the pillow, light
as a feather when we lie in love's
weather, but tonight I sleep alone,
the closet full of skeletons that grin
in the chilly breeze. Starving,
they climb love's zero by degrees,
as I will, the pillow dreaming
furious dreams. Dreams not my own.

ELIZABETH SPIRES (b. 1952)

I Know

The definition of beauty is easy; it is what leads to desperation
—Valéry

I know the moon is troubling;

Its pale eloquence is always such a meddling,
Intrusive lie. I know the pearl sheen of the sheets
Remains the screen I'll draw back against the night;

I know all of those silences invented for me approximate
Those real silences I cannot lose to daylight . . .
I know the orchid smell of your skin

The way I know the blackened path to the marina,
When gathering clouds obscure the summer moon—
Just as I know the chambered heart where I begin.

I know too the lacquered jewel box, its obsidian patina;
The sexual trumpeting of the diving, sweeping loons . . .
I know the slow combinations of the night, & the glow

Of fireflies, deepening the shadows of all I do not know.

DAVID ST. JOHN (b. 1949)

Exile

The widow refuses sleep, for sleep pretends
that it can bring him back.
In this way,
the will is set against the appetite.
Even the empty hand moves to the mouth.
Apart from you,
I turn a corner in the city and find,
for a moment, the old climate,
the little blue flower everywhere.

ELLEN BRYANT VOIGT (b. 1943)

from Let Me Think

You ask me about that country
whose details now escape me.
I don't remember its geography,
nothing of its history.
And should I visit it in memory,
it would be as I would a past lover,
after years, for a night,
no longer restless with passion,
     with no fear of regret.
I have reached that age
when one visits the heart
     merely as a courtesy . . .

FAIZ AHMED FAIZ (1911–1984)
Translated from the Urdu by Agha Shahid Ali

Meeting at Night

The gray sea and the long black land;
And the yellow half-moon large and low;
And the startled little waves that leap
In fiery ringlets from their sleep,
As I gain the cove with pushing prow,
And quench its speed i' the slushy sand.

Then a mile of warm sea-scented beach;
Three fields to cross till a farm appears;
A tap at the pane, the quick sharp scratch
And blue spurt of a lighted match,
And a voice less loud, through its joys and fears,
Than the two hearts beating each to each!

ROBERT BROWNING (1812–1889)

Water Can Only Wrap Me, but Life Must Hold Me

A Black man, from Oklahoma,
Married moisture.
Her name was Ruth.

Whenever he talked a stone
Cracked for water,
But not for doom.

Over the years she has become
Sweeter, listening
Like a horned toad:
At nights,
Wearing only her own
Horned toad clothes—
But breathing

As strong as they fit her.

It has been years . . .
Love and exposure have become a poem.

PRIMUS ST. JOHN (b. 1939)

139

from **Variation on the Word *Sleep***

I would like to be the air
that inhabits you for a moment
only. I would like to be that unnoticed
& that necessary.

MARGARET ATWOOD (b. 1939)

Sonnet XVII

I don't love you as if you were the salt-rose, topaz
or arrow of carnations that propagate fire:
I love you as certain dark things are loved,
secretly, between the shadow and the soul.

I love you as the plant that doesn't bloom and carries
hidden within itself the light of those flowers,
and thanks to your love, darkly in my body
lives the dense fragrance that rises from the earth.

I love you without knowing how, or when, or from where,
I love you simply, without problems or pride:
I love you in this way because I don't know any other way of loving

but this, in which there is no I or you,

so intimate that your hand upon my chest is my hand,
so intimate that when I fall asleep it is your eyes that close.

PABLO NERUDA (1904–1973)
Translated from the Spanish by Stephen Mitchell

from Watch Repair

A small wheel
Incandescent,
Shivering like
A pinned butterfly.

Hands thrown up
In all directions:
The crossroads
One arrives at
In a nightmare.

Higher than that
Number 12 presides
Like a beekeeper

Over the swarming honeycomb
Of the open watch.

CHARLES SIMIC (b. 1938)

144

The Poem

It discovers by night
what the day hid from it.
Sometimes it turns itself
into an animal.
In summer it takes long walks
by itself where meadows
fold back from ditches.
Once it stood still
in a quiet row of machines.
Who knows
what it is thinking?

DONALD HALL (b. 1928)

Say Uncle

Every day
you say,
Just one
more try.
Then another
irrecoverable
day slips by.
You will
say *ankle,*
you will
say *knuckle,*
why won't
you why
won't you
say *uncle*?

KAY RYAN (b. 1945)

The Well Dressed Man with a Beard

After the final no there comes a yes
And on that yes the future world depends.
No was the night. Yes is this present sun.
If the rejected things, the things denied,
Slid over the western cataract, yet one,
One only, one thing that was firm, even
No greater than a cricket's horn, no more
Than a thought to be rehearsed all day, a speech
Of the self that must sustain itself on speech,
One thing remaining, infallible, would be
Enough. Ah! douce campagna of that thing!
Ah! douce campagna, honey in the heart,
Green in the body, out of a petty phrase,
Out of a thing believed, a thing affirmed:
The form on the pillow humming while one sleeps,

The aureole above the humming house . . .

It can never be satisfied, the mind, never.

WALLACE STEVENS (1879–1955)

from **The Tyger**

When the stars threw down their spears
And water'd heaven with their tears,
Did he smile his work to see?
Did he who made the Lamb make thee?

Tyger! Tyger! burning bright
In the forests of the night,
What immortal hand or eye,
Dare frame thy fearful symmetry?

WILLIAM BLAKE (1757–1827)

from **They Feed They Lion**

From my five arms and all my hands,
From all my white sins forgiven, they feed,
From my car passing under the stars,
They Lion, from my children inherit,
From the oak turned to a wall, they Lion,
From they sack and they belly opened
And all that was hidden burning on the oil-stained earth
They feed they Lion and he comes.

PHILIP LEVINE (b. 1928)

When I Heard the Learn'd Astronomer

When I heard the learn'd astronomer,
When the proofs, the figures, were ranged in columns before me,
When I was shown the charts and diagrams, to add, divide, and measure them,
When I sitting heard the astronomer where he lectured with much applause
      in the lecture-room,
How soon unaccountable I became tired and sick,
Till rising and gliding out I wander'd off by myself,
In the mystical moist night-air, and from time to time,
Look'd up in perfect silence at the stars.

WALT WHITMAN (1819–1892)

acknowledgments

Poetry in Motion from Coast to Coast is a collaboration among numerous individuals, organizations, and institutions. We owe immense gratitude to the inspiration, suggestions, generosity, and hard work of many.

We would like to thank the Board of Governors of the Poetry Society of America—in particular, Molly Peacock, a co-founder of *Poetry in Motion* and former PSA President, William Louis-Dreyfus, PSA's current President, as well as Ellen Rachlin and Howard Rothman. Special thanks to Alice Quinn, Executive Director, whose dedication will ensure the future of the *Poetry in Motion* program, as well as to the industrious staff of the PSA, including Eve Grubin, Michael Haskell, Rachel Cohen, Jennifer Kronovet, and Stefania Heim, and to previous staff members Cynthia Atkins, Diana Burnham, Jeffrey Lependorf, Michele Miller, and Susan Sully. We owe many thanks to the past *Poetry in Motion* coordinators, including Timothy Donnelly, Matthew Rohrer, and Andrew Zawacki.

We are grateful to the poets and publishers who have generously agreed to have their poems reprinted in the program.

Thanks to the National Endowment for the Arts and Cliff Becker; and the Lila Wallace–*Reader's Digest* Fund and Sheila Murphy and Holly Sidford, for enabling the PSA to make *Poetry in Motion* a national program.

The New York City program was launched in 1992, thanks to the inspiration of Alan F. Kiepper, President (1990–1996), MTA New York City Transit, who set the wheels of poetry in motion; thanks also to NYC Transit President Lawrence G. Reuter; Thomas J. Savage, Senior Vice President, Department of MetroCard Operations; and Alicia Martinez, Director of Marketing and Corporate Communications, for their continued enthusiastic support of the program; and to Neil Neches, Marketing Manager for NYC Transit. The program would not be possible without generous contributions from Barnes & Noble, Inc.; the New York State Council on the Arts and Kathleen Masterson; the New York City Department of Cultural Affairs; the Robert Sterling Clark Foundation; the Gladys Krieble Delmas Foundation; the Viburnum Foundation; and the Manhattan Delegation to the New York City Council.

We are indebted to the American Institute of Graphic Arts (AIGA) and to all the designers in cities across the country who donated their time in the creation of posters. Particular thanks to former PSA Vice President and former AIGA President Bill Drentell.

Thanks, also, to those individuals and organizations for their help in developing *Poetry in Motion* in cities nationwide:

The Chicago program, launched in 1996, and presented in association with the Chicago Transit Authority with Noelle Gaffney and Marisue O'Connor; AIGA/Chicago with Bill Hafeman,

Mark Oldach, and Vernon Lockhart; the Chicago Public Library with Mary Dempsey and Gerry Keane; former PSA Board member G. E. Murray; Petrick Design; Lake County Press; Jet Lithocolor, Inc.; Potlatch Corporation; the Joyce Foundation; Richard H. Driehaus Foundation; the Irving Harris Foundation; the Sara Lee Foundation; the Chicago Community Trust; Barnes & Noble, Inc.; the Illinois Arts Council; and Mead Paper Corporation.

The Boston program, launched in 1996, and presented in association with Massachusetts Bay Transportation Authority with Maurice Lewis and Bob O'Brien; AIGA/Boston with Paul Montee, Denise Korn and Cheryl Bricker; Bonnie McLellan and South Station's Beacon Management; Tree Swenson; Unisource; Graphics Express; Calendar Press; and Laserscan.

The Baltimore program, launched in 1997, and presented in association with AIGA/Baltimore with Carl Cox, President, Baltimore Chapter; Trish Cerbelli, Meghan Alonzo, and Caryn Radlove; the Maryland Mass Transit Administration with Pam Goins-Watts; Maryland Department of Transportation; the Enoch Pratt Free Library with Judy Cooper and Teresa Edmunds; J. W. Boarman Co., Inc., and Rob Close; Rainbow Lithography of Maryland; WWF Paper Company; Zanders; Scheufelen; and Elizabeth Spires.

The Portland program, launched in 1997, and presented in association with Literary Arts Inc. with Carrie Hoops and Lara Utman; Tri-Met; Obie Media; AIGA/Portland; Portland State University Center for Excellence in Writing; the Oregon Community Foundation; Portland State University Department of English; Regional Arts and Culture Council; Starbucks Coffee; and Dietrich Coffee People.

The Atlanta program, launched in 1998, and presented in association with Metropolitan Atlanta Rapid Transit Authority; AIGA/Atlanta; Mead Paper Corporation; and Graphic Arts Center.

The Dallas program, launched in 1998, and presented in association with Dallas Area Rapid Transit; Richland College/Dallas County Community College District; and Program Coordinator Martha Heimberg.

The Los Angeles program, launched in 1998, and presented in association with the Metro Art Department of the Los Angeles County Metropolitan Transportation Authority with Maya Emsden; and the Getty Research Institute for the History of Art and the Humanities with JoEllen Williamson, Karen Sexton-Josephs, and Charles Salas. The 2000–1 series was presented in association with the LACMTA with in-kind support from Pamela Mass Design. Special thanks are extended to PSA in LA Director Elena Karina Byrne.

The Washington, D.C., program, launched in 1998, and presented in association with Washington Metropolitan Area Transit Authority with Gwendolyn Mitchell, Brett Tyler, Randy Howes, Marilyn Dicus, and Cheryl Johnson; AIGA/Washington D.C. with Hannah Smotrich, Tamera Lawrence, and Sam Shelton; International Paper; Peake Printers; and PSB Imaging.

The Philadelphia program, launched in 1999, and presented in association with AIGA/Philadelphia and Rosemary Murphy; the Southeastern Pennsylvania Transit Authority and Barbara Siegel in Media Relations; John Cooley and all of Innovation Printing and Lithography; Karen Eddows; and the Mead Paper Corporation.

The Pioneer Valley program, launched in 2000, presented in association with Pioneer Valley

Transit Authority with Gary Shepard and Tammie Poulos; UMASS Amherst with Rob Casper, Lisa Olstein, Christopher Janke, and Dara Wier; and MassLive with Sue Lutz.

The Austin program, launched in 2000, and presented in association with AIGA/Austin with Heather Brand, Dave Holston, and Sherri Whitmarsh; Borderlands: *Texas Poetry Review*; the Austin Transit Authority; and Obie Media.

The Fort Collins program, launched in 2000, and presented in association with Colorado State University and Mary Crow.

The Houston program, launched in 2000, and presented in association with the Metropolitan Transit Authority of Harris County, Texas, with Barbara McKinney and Leigh Anne Patterson; and program coordinator Julie Fernandez.

The Iowa program, launched in 2000, and presented in association with MTA Des Moines; Iowa City Transit; Scan Graphics, Inc.; AIGA/Iowa and program coordinator Melinda Schulte; the Des Moines Poetry Society and Jay Johnson; Lessing-Flynn Advertising and Marla Hall-Fay; and the Iowa City Public Library.

The Ohio State program, launched in 2000, and presented in association with the Ohio State Transportation and Parking Services; University Marketing Communications; the OSU University Honors and Scholars Center; OSU Creative Writing Program; and Yaegar Graphics.

We also are indebted to Hillel Parness for his legal expertise, Fred Courtright for his permissions advice, Kathleen Anderson for representing the PSA, and Carol Houck Smith for her commitment to poetry.

about the editors

Elise Paschen, a co-founder of the *Poetry in Motion* program, served as the Executive Director of the Poetry Society of America from 1988–2001. She is the author of two books of poems, *Infidelities,* winner of the Nicholas Roerich Poetry Prize; and *Houses: Coasts*; and co-editor of the anthologies *Poetry in Motion* and *Poetry Speaks.* Dr. Paschen currently teaches in the Writing Program at the School of the Art Institute of Chicago.

Brett Fletcher Lauer is the *Poetry in Motion* Director for the Poetry Society of America and the Assistant Managing Editor of Verse Press. His poems have appeared in *Boston Review, Denver Quarterly*, and *Slope.*

permissions

Lucille Clifton, "whose side are you on?" from *quilting: poems 1987–1990.* Copyright © 1991 by Lucille Clifton. Reprinted with the permission of BOA Editions, Ltd.

Wanda Coleman, "False Spring" from *Hand Dance.* Copyright © 1993 by Wanda Coleman. Reprinted with the permission of Black Sparrow Press.

Michael Collier, "The Heavy Light of Shifting Stars" (excerpt) from *The Folded Heart.* Copyright © 1989 by Michael Collier. Reprinted with the permission of Wesleyan University Press.

Billy Collins, "Hunger" from *The Apple that Astonished Paris.* Copyright © 1988 by Billy Collins. Reprinted with the permission of the University of Arkansas Press.

Peter Davison, "Peaches" from *The Great Ledge.* Copyright © 1989 by Peter Davison. Reprinted with the permission of Alfred A. Knopf, a division of Random House, Inc.

Toi Derricotte, "The Good Old Dog" from *Captivity.* Copyright © 1989 by Toi Derricotte. Reprinted with the permission of the University of Pittsburgh Press.

Paul Laurence Dunbar, "Sympathy" (excerpt) from *The Collected Poems of Paul Laurence Dunbar,* edited by Joanne M. Braxton. Copyright © 1993. Reprinted with the permission of the University of Virginia Press.

Faiz Ahmed Faiz, "Let Me Think" (excerpt) translated by Agha Shahid Ali, from *The Rebel's Silhouette.* Copyright © 1991 by the University of Massachusetts Press. Reprinted with the permission of the publisher.

James Fenton, "The Ideal" from *Out of Danger.* Copyright © 1994 by James Fenton. Reprinted with the permission of Farrar, Straus and Giroux, LLC.

Calvin Forbes, "The Potter's Wheel" from *Blue Monday.* Copyright © 1974 by Calvin Forbes. Reprinted with the permission of the author.

Robert Frost, "Mending Wall" (excerpt) from *The Poetry of Robert Frost,* edited by Edward Connery Lathem. Copyright © 1969 by Henry Holt and Company. Reprinted with the permission of Henry Holt & Company, LLC.

Nan Fry, "Riddle" from *Relearning the Dark.* Copyright © 1991 by Nan Fry. Reprinted with the permission of the author and Washington Writers' Publishing House.

Tu Fu, "Too Much Heat, Too Much Work" translated by Carolyn Kizer, from *Cool, Calm & Collected: Poems 1960–2000.* Copyright © 2001 by Carolyn Kizer. Reprinted with the permission of Copper Canyon Press, PO Box 271, Port Townsend, WA 98368-0271.

Gloria Fuertes, "Painted Windows" translated by Philip Levine. Reprinted with the permission of the translator.

N. Scott Momaday, "The Gift" from *Gourd Dance*. Copyright © 1976 by N. Scott Momaday. Reprinted with the permission of the author.

Lisel Mueller, "Love Like Salt" from *Alive Together: New and Selected Poems*. Copyright © 1996 by Lisel Mueller. Reprinted with the permission of Louisiana State University Press.

Paul Muldoon, "The Sonogram" from *The Annals of Chile*. Copyright © 1994 by Paul Muldoon. Reprinted with the permission of Farrar, Straus and Giroux, LLC.

Carol Muske-Dukes, "Little L.A. Villanelle" (excerpt) from *An Octave Above Thunder*. Copyright © 1997 by Carol Muske-Dukes. Reprinted with the permission of Penguin, a division of Penguin Putnam, Inc.

Isabel Nathaniel, "On the Patio, Dallas" from *The Dominion of Lights*. Copyright © 1996 by Isabel Nathaniel. Reprinted with the permission of Copper Beech Press.

Pablo Neruda, "Sonnet XVII" translated by Stephen Mitchell, from *Full Woman, Fleshly Apple, Hot Moon*. Copyright © 1997 by Stephen Mitchell. Reprinted with the permission of the University of Texas Press.

Nino Nikolov, "Confusion" translated by Ewald Osers, from *Contemporary East European Poetry: An Anthology*, edited by Emery George. Copyright © 1993 by Emery George. Reprinted with the permission of the translator.

John Frederick Nims, "Days of Our Years" from *Zany in Denim*. Copyright © 1990 by John Frederick Nims. Reprinted with the permission of Bonnie Nims and the University of Arkansas Press.

Naomi Shihab Nye, "Open House" from *Fuel*. Copyright © 1998 by Naomi Shihab Nye. Reprinted with the permission of BOA Editions, Ltd.

Sharon Olds, "Primitive" from *Satan Says*. Copyright © 1980 by Sharon Olds. Reprinted with the permission of the University of Pittsburgh Press.

Mary Oliver, "The Loon on Oak-Head Pond" from *House of Light*. Copyright © 1990 by Mary Oliver. Reprinted with the permission of Beacon Press.

Alicia Partnoy, "Communication" from *Revenge of the Apple/Venganza de la manzana*. Copyright © 1992 by Alicia Partnoy. Translated by Richard Schaaf, Regina Kreger, and the author. Reprinted with the permission of the author.

Robert Pinsky, "First Early Mornings Together" from *Sadness and Happiness*. Copyright © 1975 by Princeton University Press. Reprinted with the permission of Princeton University Press.

Stanley Plumly, "Wrong Side of the River" from *Out-of-the-Body Travel*. Copyright © 1974 by Stanley Plumly. Reprinted with the permission of the author.

Exit only
when directed

index of poets and translators